DREAMS
INTERPRETED

Revised edition copyright © Summersdale Publishers Ltd, 2018, 2019.

First Published by Summersdale Publishers Ltd, an imprint of Hachette UK, in 2016 as Dreamopedia.

First Skyhorse Publishing edition, 2019.

Text by Anna Martin
With thanks to Hannah Adams

Skyhorse Publishing books may be purchased in bulk at special discounts for sales promotion, corporate gifts, fund-raising, or educational purposes. Special editions can also be created to specifications. For details, contact the Special Sales Department, Skyhorse Publishing, 307 West 36th Street, 11th Floor, New York, NY 10018 or info@skyhorsepublishing.com.

Skyhorse® and Skyhorse Publishing® are registered trademarks of Skyhorse Publishing, Inc.®, a Delaware corporation.

Visit our website at www.skyhorsepublishing.com.

10 9 8 7 6 5 4 3 2 1

Library of Congress Cataloging-in-Publication Data is available on file.

ISBN: 978-1-63158-435-0
E-Book ISBN: 978-1-63158-444-2

Printed in China

DREAMS
INTERPRETED

A BEDSIDE HANDBOOK EXPLAINING EVERYTHING FROM ACCORDIONS AND ACORNS TO ZEBRAS AND ZIPPERS

Lizzie Cornwall

Skyhorse Publishing

CONTENTS

In dreams, we enter a world that's entirely our own.

—Steve Kloves

INTRODUCTION

Dreams—we have them every night, and yet they are so mysterious. They are packed with the strangest, most gripping imagery, but then they slip away from us as we wake. Dream interpretation can be used as a form of therapy—the mind has a way of unearthing memories and experiences within our dreams to help us come to terms with them, allowing us to connect with the more hidden aspects of our psyche and in turn resolve issues in our waking life. Their meanings can be discovered by interpreting the symbols contained within them.

This little book is packed with suggestions about what your dreams might mean, along with facts about sleep and dreaming to help you understand your night-time thoughts even better, and offers ways to improve your chances of remembering your dreams.

Enjoy finding out about the world of sleep, and have sweet dreams!

DO WE ALL DREAM?

According to researchers at the Lucidity Institute, we all dream throughout the night, with approximately one dream every 90 minutes. The shortest dream occurs at the beginning of a night's sleep and lasts for around ten minutes, while dreams towards the end of a night's sleep can be up to an hour long. Dreams most often occur when we experience the active stage of sleep known as rapid eye movement (REM) sleep. It's called this because one of the characteristics of REM sleep is the eyes darting under the lids at high speed. It is believed that REM sleep helps the brain to consolidate memories and plays an important role in learning, as the brain is as active as when we are conscious. Over the course of the night, our sleep patterns shift with progressively longer periods of REM sleep.

Researchers have discovered that the thought processes that enable us to recall memories shut down when we sleep, thus preventing us from being able to remember most of our dreams. The dreams that we most often remember are the ones that illicit a strong emotional reaction causing us to wake up (such as nightmares) as they can rouse us from sleep and cause the feelings to remain with us for a long time afterwards.

WAYS TO IMPROVE DREAM RECALL

It can be frustrating to awaken from the most wonderful dream, only for it to slip from your memory as you try to recall the details. If you want to improve your chances of remembering your dreams, try these ideas:

- Decide before you go to bed that you want to remember them—even speaking your intention out loud can help.

- Make your bedroom conducive to quality sleep, such as having a freshly made bed and no light pollution or gadgets that could interrupt sleep.

- Keep a pen and a notebook beside your bed, ready to write down everything that you can remember about your dreams. There's no need to write an essay; if it's the middle of the night, just jot down a couple of words, perhaps noting how the dream made you feel or a notable image. These notes will jog your memory and may even help the dream to return so that you can relive it.

● We are more likely to remember our dreams if we wake up during the dream. Set an alarm clock to rouse you earlier than you would normally wake, and you should improve your chances of remembering your dreams. Once awake, concentrate on the dream, don't think about getting up or moving around, and allow the dream to return.

LUCID DREAMING

This refers to a type of dreaming where you're aware that you are dreaming and able to exert influence on what happens within the dream. Some advocates of lucid dreaming claim during this state they are able to find solutions to problems in their waking life or spend time, albeit virtually, with people they love. It's a curious concept that has been pondered since ancient times, from the Greek philosopher Aristotle who once said, "For often, when one is asleep, there is something in consciousness which declares that what then presents itself is but a dream," right up until the present day with the lucid dream sequences in the 2010 film *Inception*.

All the limitations that you experience in real life no longer exist in lucid dreams—you can have super powers, visit the bottom of the sea or the outer reaches of space, defeat your enemies, or meet your heroes. According to research undertaken by the University of Northampton, over half the population have experienced lucid dreaming, and it tends to be those who are more insightful and self-aware than others, but there are ways in which you can teach yourself to experience them. Dream experts recommend the following steps to experience a lucid dream:

1 State your intention before you go to bed that you want to dream.

2 Before you drift off, perform some self-awareness "reality" checks, such as looking at your hand and trying to push a finger into your palm.

3 Set your alarm to wake you an hour earlier than your normal wake-up time, so that you are roused during REM sleep.

4 When you're awakened by your alarm, turn off the alarm and then wake up without opening your eyes—this is the difficult part. Allow your body to relax into sleep once more while your mind remains

active. You will experience sleep paralysis, which is when your body is temporarily paralyzed. This can be alarming when you first experience it, but it is completely normal and safe.

5   You will begin to dream again and have control over your actions within the dream. Try to push your finger into your palm—if you are lucid dreaming, it will go straight through!

6   Control your dreams by stating your intentions with clear instructions, such as, "I want to open this door to find myself on a tropical beach." Try to populate the dream with as much sensory detail as you can.

7   On waking, record everything you can remember— the smells, tastes, sounds, and textures as well as what you have seen.

Food for sweet dreams

Dreams occur during REM sleep. Certain foods can help and hinder the quality of REM sleep; for example, caffeinated drinks can upset sleeping patterns, so try to avoid these at least two hours before bed. Eating melatonin-rich foods will improve your chances of a good night's sleep and having vivid dreams. Almonds, cherries, tomatoes, seeds, and oats all contain good levels of melatonin.

Dream dictionary
A–Z

This A–Z of meanings contains some of the most common symbols and experiences in dreams. Our dreams use symbolism to speak; it is a secret code that is not based on the direct associations we make when we are awake. The symbols that we see in our dreams often bring about an idea or emotion in a strong way. This means that when we sleep we may be able to uncover hidden feelings, meaning, and ideas.

Don't worry too much if the interpretations given in these pages don't match your own experiences—everyone's dreams are unique and their meanings are special for the individual, so use the meanings as a starting point to discover what your subconscious mind is trying to tell you.

ABANDONMENT

Being abandoned in a dream can be unnerving and nightmarish at the time and it may relate to a recent ending of something important, such as a relationship or work situation. It could also be tuning in to feelings of neglect as a child or in a grown-up relationship. Another interpretation is that you might be a great starter of things, but you have a tendency to lose momentum and leave things unfinished.

ACCIDENT

To dream that you have an accident may signify pent-up guilt for which you are subconsciously punishing yourself. Perhaps you are not proud of something you have done? Alternatively, the accident may symbolize an error or mistake you have made due to not feeling sufficiently in control of a situation. It's fear that tends to make us feel that we are not in control, so try to think about the area of your life that is causing you stress and work to alleviate it in order to regain calm and focus.

ACCORDION

If you dream that you are playing an accordion, it means that something in your life is causing you to feel very unhappy and it's putting a lot of physical strain on you. Equally, if you hear the sound of an accordion in your dream, it implies that you need to focus your attentions on the happier, more positive aspects of your life—perhaps you should take up a musical instrument, but maybe not the accordion...

ACORNS

To see an acorn in your dream symbolizes new beginnings and a fresh start, and the possibility of a new venture dominating your life, but in a positive way. Seeing acorns dropping to the ground implies that you have great influence on others.

ADDRESS

Dreaming about a place you used to live or a place you used to frequent hints that you will shortly come into contact with someone from your past, and in a most unusual way—perhaps you will find yourself sitting next to an ex-partner on a train, or you'll accidently dig up your dead hamster when planting bulbs.

I've dreamt in my life,
dreams that have stayed with
me ever after, and changed
my ideas; they've gone
through and through
me, like wine through
water, and altered the
color of my mind.

—Emily Brontë

ADVENTURE

Dreaming of having adventures in exotic climes could mean your daily life has become a bit stale. Perhaps it's time to book that trek up Kilimanjaro or register for the Marathon des Sables to help you rediscover your zest for life.

AGE

Dreaming that you're older than you actually are hints that you have regrets about not trying a certain way of living, but luckily it's not too late to take a risk. Dreaming that you are younger implies that a more have-a-go, carefree attitude is called for, so make the most of the opportunities that come your way.

AIRPLANE

Planes soaring through the sky in your dream signify that any current setbacks or obstacles will soon be overcome and you'll make great headway in your plans. If your dream is about a plane taking off, a project dear to you is likely to soon get off the ground.

ALIEN

Seeing an extraterrestrial in your dream means that you feel alienated from a person or a place and are struggling to come to terms with these feelings. See *UFO*.

Dream fact

We break the rules in our sleep and often our wildest fantasies come to play in our dream worlds. Interestingly, it is said that even while sleeping our brains are aware of how few consequences there are for our imagined actions.

BABIES

To dream of babies doesn't necessarily mean that you are feeling broody. Babies are symbols of purity and innocence, and in some cases, vulnerability. If the baby is smiling at you, then you can hope for a moment of pure joy or a new beginning.

BACKFLIPS

Dreaming of doing backflips means that you are bending over backwards to accommodate or please someone in your waking life and it's not really producing the results that you'd hoped for. It's time to try a different tack— make them do the backflips instead!

BAD BREATH

If people are noticing that you have bad breath in your dream, it means that you need to learn to think before you speak, and consider the power of words and how they affect others.

Dream fact

It is said that we only dream about familiar faces. The faces that we see in our dreams are either of people that we know, or of people we have seen in passing and perhaps have stored deep in our subconscious.

BEING CHASED

This is a common anxiety dream. First try to remember who or what is chasing you to gain a better understanding of what it is that you are worried about. Also consider the distance between you and what is chasing you—if the chaser is close by then you are feeling overwhelmed by a situation, whereas if the chaser is a significant distance away this suggests you will conquer your current problems with ease. These dreams are also common if you watch the news or a scary movie before going to bed.

BETRAYAL

This means that you feel very insecure about a situation, possibly with a partner or colleague, and you are suspicious of their motives or worried they may be doing things that could damage your relationship.

BICYCLE

Riding a bicycle portents a period of personal growth and development, and because you are powering the bicycle under your own steam, these changes will happen at a comfortable pace.

BIRDCAGE

This is quite a common dream about self-expression. It can mean that you are experiencing a loss of freedom—not necessarily on a sinister level; you could have just got married or had a baby, for example, and are settling into a different way of living where you have to consider the needs of another person before making decisions.

BIRDS

Birds represent your ambitions, hopes, and desires, and it's especially good news if they are chirping happily as these personal goals will come to fruition. If the birds appear to be fighting, however, it means that you have too many irons in the fire or are spreading yourself too thinly, which could result in you missing the mark and ending up on a less-desirable path. See *Flying*.

All that we see or seem is but a dream within a dream.

—Edgar Allan Poe

BLINDNESS

To be blind in your dream hints that there might be a lack of self-awareness in your life that is muddying your ability to acknowledge a persistent problem. It's time to take a look at the thing that you are perpetually avoiding and deal with it so you can be your best self once more.

BREAKING THE LAW

If you dream that you're a criminal or coerced into a criminal act, then it's likely that you are under the influence of someone who doesn't have your best interests at heart and may be encouraging you to behave badly; it's time to follow your own path not someone else's.

CABBAGE

If you dream of eating cabbage, or seeing some, you could be about to receive a proposal or a new challenge—it's up to you if you take it. If the cabbage tastes bad or has a moldy appearance, saying yes to these new opportunities could be unwise.

–(–

CABLE CAR

Riding in a cable car and being surrounded by a wonderful view means that you are generally happy with the direction in which your life is heading.

CACTI

Dreaming of these prickly plants means that you feel suffocated by the constraints placed on your life. It could be that you have a very dictatorial boss or your partner's behavior is leaving a lot to be desired. It's time to break out of this cycle and lay down the law, or just walk away and find a better situation.

CAKE

Seeing, buying, or consuming cakes in your dream hints that you need to learn to prioritize commitments and restrict the time you spend on certain activities. It could also mean that you're giving too much of your time to others and you need to take some back before you become resentful. Have some "me" time—eat cake!

Dream fact

Not everyone dreams in color. It is said that 12 percent of us dream in black and white. However, since the advent of color television more and more of us dream in color.

CAMPING

This means a break is long overdue, preferably one where you reconnect with nature and that allows you to focus on the simple things in life. A campfire denotes a need for companionship and a desire to extend your social circle.

CANDLE

A glowing candle signifies good luck. It also means that you have reached a stage of contentment but have a burning desire to learn about the more spiritual side of life. If the candle blows out, this suggests an aspect of your life is about to change significantly and the impact will be far-reaching.

CHRISTMAS

First consider your own thoughts about the festive season: if you find it stressful, dreaming about Christmas could mean that you are anxious about an event that is coming up; if it's a time that you look forward to because of the social and family-oriented aspects, then perhaps you need to ring someone you love for a good chat.

CLIMBING

This is often associated with metaphorically scaling obstacles to achieve a cherished dream. If you succeeded in reaching the summit, it means you have confidence in your abilities to get to where you want to be, but if you found yourself stuck and unable to move up or down, it might mean that you need to revisit your strategy as it could be unrealistic and require a rethink.

The future belongs to those who believe in the beauty of their dreams.

—Eleanor Roosevelt

ARTEMIDORUS, ONEIROCRITICA (c. CE 2)

In the second century AD, a professional diviner from Ephesus by the name of Artemidorus Daldianus wrote the *Oneirocritica* (from the Greek *oneiro* "dream" and *kritikon* "interpretation").

Artemidorus suggested that dreams were unique to the individual, and that a person's waking life would affect the symbols in their dreams. It was also suggested that there were two main types of dream, the first of which he called *enhypnia* and these could be prompted by bodily needs and recent real-life events. The second type of dream foretold the future, either prophetically or in response to prayer.

Each of the five books of the *Oneirocritica* divides dreams into groups, such as dreams that include the anatomy and activity of the human body, events in the natural world, and miscellaneous happenings. An

interpretation in one of these books states that if a poor man dreams of gold, it is a prediction that he will become rich, while if a rich man were to dream of gold, he was going to be scammed; such was the role that an individual's life played in the meaning of a dream.

DEATH

To dream of a death is not as final as it may first appear. It symbolizes change, or at least a desire for something positive to happen. It can foresee a period of change, such as a new job or house move, or a new relationship, so it can be one of the more positive things to dream about. See *Dying*.

DEVIL

The devil signifies that you are being deceived in some way or unwittingly drawn into something that doesn't sit well with you. The deceiver is likely to be an intelligent member of your friendship circle. It's time to wake up, reset your moral compass, and scout out some less devilish friends.

DOGS

It's important to reflect on what the dog is doing in order to interpret the dream correctly. If the dog is baring its teeth like it may bite you, it means that you are struggling to reconcile something within yourself. Alternatively, if the dog is friendly, then your social life is taking an upturn. A barking dog implies that you can be a little overbearing—bark less and smile more.

DOOR

Entering a door suggests you have some golden opportunities coming your way. An open door means that you are particularly receptive to new ideas, whereas if the door is locked, you might be feeling shut out or overlooked. If you are locking the door, you could be closing yourself off from others.

DRAGON

These mythical, lizard-like creatures suggest that you have a combustible personality—a short fuse—which could be causing problems with your nearest and dearest. Calm down and deal with this now or you might end up out in the cold.

DRIVING

If you are in the driver's seat, you need to consider how you are driving—whether responsibly or recklessly—as this denotes your approach to life. If you encounter obstacles or difficult driving conditions, it could mean that you are struggling to come to terms with difficulties that you are facing in your waking life. If you're driving in blizzard conditions, it means you need to take extra care when dealing with situations that you'll soon face. If you are the passenger in the car, this could mean you feel powerless and it's time to claw back some of the responsibilities and control that you previously enjoyed. See *Vehicle*.

DROWNING

This dream can be very unsettling, and it means that you are feeling swamped with responsibilities and struggling to cope with the demands being made of you. If you pull yourself to safety or are rescued, you will soon begin to feel better able to cope with your current situation—hang in there.

DYING

To dream that you are dying implies that you are in a negative situation in your life—such as a toxic relationship or you've made an unhealthy lifestyle choice—and it's a wake-up call to do something about it. It doesn't mean that your life is at risk, but you are likely to be feeling unhappy or out of sorts with your current situation. If you dream that you have died, this is actually much more positive as it signifies transformation and new beginnings—out with the old and in with the new. See *Death*.

EARTH

The Earth represents a feeling of stability and calm, but to dream about it signifies the opposite—you feel unsettled and anxious. It's time to get back to basics and become more grounded and at one with the earth and the people that you love.

EARWIG

These wriggly creatures are a bad omen as they imply that you will receive news that could rattle you—it could be something related to either work or home. You can't keep bad news at bay, just as you can't keep insects out of your home.

ECLIPSE

To witness an eclipse in your dream means you are fearful that you will not achieve the goals you have set yourself. It could also signify that you have lost your way and are feeling left in the dark. If the eclipse passes in your dream, you will soon find a new way to tackle your goals.

EGGS

This classic fertility dream isn't necessarily about wishing for a baby; it can also mean the birth of a creative enterprise, especially if the eggs are hatching. A nest filled with eggs is a portent to financial gain. To dream that the eggs are cracked suggests that you feel vulnerable and you need to develop a thicker skin.

ELDERLY

Old people can symbolize wisdom. If you see an old person in your dream, are they trying to guide you or help you with a decision you have to make? Check the way this person behaves, as this can reflect your feelings about aging. Seeing a healthy, happy old person suggests you feel positive about the prospect of growing older.

ELEPHANT

Whether they're pink elephants in tutus or ones roaming the wild, these mighty creatures symbolize your personal power, be it physical, intellectual, or spiritual. Elephants never forget, apparently, and therefore your dream could be interpreted that you are holding on to an outmoded belief or relationship and it may be time to move on and sign up for a dating app.

ELEVATOR

Try to remember whether you were going up or down in the elevator as this makes a big difference to the interpretation. If the elevator is going up, it means you could see a dramatic rise in wealth and status—so much so that you are a little fearful of the responsibilities this brings. If the elevator is going down, then setbacks or even a financial loss could be imminent. If you are trapped in the elevator, then your dream is telling you that your life is spiraling out of control and you need to regroup and go back to square one.

EXAMS

This is a very common dream, especially one where you are sitting an exam and you can't understand or answer the questions on the paper. That horrible feeling of being unprepared and out of your depth may mirror something coming up in your life that you don't feel ready for. If this is the case, start planning and take steps to help you relax before the big day.

EXPLOSIONS

To witness an explosion means that you are suppressing feelings of anger and it's time to let it out before it causes emotional damage. Find a friend to confide in or just run up to the highest point and scream bloody murder.

We are such stuff as dreams are made on and our little life is rounded with a sleep.

—William Shakespeare

FACE

If you see your own face in your dream, as if looking in the mirror, this represents the side of you that you show the world—your public persona and how you think people see you. If the skin is cracking on your face, it means that any deceptions are about to be uncovered. If your face is swollen, you could be about to see an upturn in your financial situation.

FAIRIES

To dream of fairy folk indicates that you are searching for answers and would like some support in negotiating a tricky decision or problem—but it might be best not to wait for your fairy godmother to appear. It also indicates that you are embracing your feminine side.

FALLING

This is a common anxiety dream symbolizing a sense of powerlessness in your life or a feeling that you're not being listened to. If you are falling backwards in your dream, it's a hint to look at a current problem from a different angle to avoid making a big mistake.

FANGS

To dream that you have fangs implies that you have said something that has proved very hurtful to someone and you need to make amends—your bark is worse than your bite.

FARTING

If you are releasing noxious emissions in your dreams, it could mean that you need to be more direct with your loved ones, rather than skirting around issues. Smelling a fart means that someone is being deceitful.

–F–

Dream fact

The Egyptians were the first to create a dream dictionary, around 1220 BCE. It is called the "Papyrus Chester Beatty 3" and was discovered in Thebes—it now resides in the British Museum.

FATHER

Dreaming of your dad or a father figure in your life suggests that you need to become more self-reliant and mature.

FIGHTING

If you are involved in a scuffle in your dream, it indicates that you are at war with yourself in some way and that you have issues that you need to resolve, ones you can no longer ignore. If you're losing the fight, it shows that you struggle with self-esteem and need to work on your inner confidence.

FLYING

The classic dream of soaring through the clouds like a bird signifies self-confidence and a happy state of mind. However, if you are dodging power lines, chimneys, and treetops mid-flight, this symbolizes obstacles to overcome in your waking life that are preventing you from moving forward, or unrealistic goals that you have set yourself. See *Birds*.

Dream fact

In 1965, Paul McCartney awoke suddenly and composed the hit song "Yesterday." He said that the melody came to him in his dream. He believed he'd dreamed of someone else's song and tried to track it down. A few weeks later, convinced that it was an original melody, he wrote the lyrics to accompany it.

Did you know...?

There are many cases where people have experienced premonitions while dreaming, such as:

★ Abraham Lincoln foresaw his own assassination in a dream.

★ Mark Twain dreamed of his own brother's passing.

★ There are many reports of large-scale catastrophes being foreseen in dreams, such as the sinking of the *Titanic* and the events of 9/11.

GARDEN

Dreaming of a lush garden indicates a steady growth towards your goals and objectives, but also a need to develop spiritually. If the garden is overgrown or full of weeds, it shows that you are neglecting your needs, and personal growth can't take place until you set aside some time for self-development.

GARLIC

Garlic has an obvious association with odor. If you dream about garlic, you may be secretly worried that you have bad breath. Vampires are another association or you may feel you need protecting from something. Finally, garlic is well known for its health benefits, which could suggest you desire greater health and well-being, and an ability to fight off illness.

GHOST

Seeing ghosts suggests that you feel disconnected from a person or a place and are unsure of how to reestablish contact. Ghosts also represent regrets or perhaps an incident from your past that you have yet to come to terms with, which is now affecting your life and needs to be dealt with.

GIFT

If you are given a gift in a dream, it could symbolize a special gift or talent that you were given at birth. Look for other clues in the dream as to what this gift or talent could be. On the other hand, if you give a gift to someone in your dream, you may need to express something to someone in a way that needs to be carefully packaged!

GIRAFFE

With their long necks, giraffes symbolize the ability to see things from a higher perspective. Is it time to look at the bigger picture? Alternatively, you may feel as if you are standing out from the crowd or sticking your neck out for someone. Tune in to how the dream made you feel to see whether you need to pull your neck in a little.

GLACIER

Glaciers represent frozen or blocked emotions. For example, you may be shutting down emotionally and having difficulty expressing your feelings. If the glacier melts in your dream, consider this a good omen—you are letting your guard down and beginning to feel your full range of emotions.

GLOVES

What sort of gloves are you wearing in your dream? Driving gloves may signify that you need to take control of your life. Work gloves may signify the need to get your hands dirty. Boxing gloves could signify conflict. Gloves can also represent the way you handle things— perhaps you are overly cautious or you need to throw more caution to the wind.

Dream fact

If it takes you less than five minutes to fall asleep, it's likely you are sleep deprived. It should take roughly 10–15 minutes to get to sleep.

GOLD

Dreaming of gold could be an auspicious sign. Gold signifies wealth and riches. Depending on the context, gold may signify things that you treasure or value in your life. It can also symbolize spirituality, inner resources, and talents. Of course, gold can also signify greed and corruption. Is there a gold-digger in your midst?

Dreams
are
necessary
to
life.

—Anaïs Nin

SIGMUND FREUD
(1856–1939)

Though his theories were published over one hundred years ago, Austrian neurologist Sigmund Freud remains one of the most influential and widely known scientists in the fields of psychology and psychiatry. Freud developed several controversial theories in his career, the most noteworthy of which was psychoanalysis. This approach focuses on how our unconscious controls our behavior and makes us act in certain ways; some of its core elements involved treatments such as free association ("the talking cure") and dream analysis.

Freud theorized that dreams acted as valuable clues to the mystery of the human psyche, and in his work *The Interpretation of Dreams,* Freud developed his methods for accessing the recesses of our minds. Freud believed that it was only once you could distinguish between the manifest content of your dream (what

a dreamer remembers) and the latent content (the symbolic meaning) that you could access your repressed experiences and desires. In his later theories of psychosexual development, Freud expanded on the origins of repression in the psyche, arguing that a failure to develop our innate and instinctual libido was the cause of most human neuroses. Freud's theories, though now widely discredited, were foundational to the psychology of dreams.

HAIL

As hail is solid ice, it can be very destructive. Dreaming of large hailstones could indicate damage in your life or the feeling that life's pressures are raining down on you. Smaller hailstones that don't do much damage might signify the need for transformation in some way.

HAIR LOSS

Hair is an important part of our identity, so dreaming of hair loss can be very significant. Men who dream of losing their hair may fear losing their strength and masculinity. Women who dream of hair loss may be anxious about their attractiveness or femininity.

HANDSHAKE

If you are shaking hands with someone in your dream, you may be about to welcome something new into your life or to begin an end to a situation. Handshakes represent deals and agreements—with yourself or someone else. Watch out for a wet, floppy handshake— your commitment might be wavering!

HAT

Depending on the context, a hat in a dream can mean all sorts of things. Ask yourself the following: are you hiding something from others? Are you fed up of wearing lots of different hats (i.e. playing different roles) in your life? Maybe you're already at your best or maybe you need to smarten up your act?

HEALING POWERS

Dreaming of healing, or being healed, suggests there may be some emotional or physical pain in your life that needs to be soothed.

HEART

The heart is the classic symbol of love and emotion. If you dream of a beating heart, try to remember if the beats were strong and robust or intermittent and quiet— the former represents confidence in your choices and that you are content with your life's path, but the latter could mean that you are not paying due attention to what's really important to you.

HEAVY

Heaviness in a dream implies some kind of burden or struggle. Is there a weight on your shoulders? Are you suffering from heavy emotions such as sadness or depression? Examine the object in your dream and how you are carrying it. Perhaps it's time to lighten up and let life flow.

HEDGEHOG

Hedgehogs are known for their ability to curl into a ball to protect themselves. Dreaming of a hedgehog suggests that you are feeling vulnerable and feel the need to defend yourself. Alternatively, your dream may be telling you to stop being so prickly!

HIPPOPOTAMUS

Dreaming of hippos suggests you are powerful and hold more sway than you realize. It could also mean that you are being territorial and need to chill out—perhaps it's time to find your own waterhole to wallow in.

Dream fact

Our brains make decisions while we sleep. The brain processes complex stimuli during a sleep state and uses this information to make decisions while we are awake... so it *is* worth sleeping on big choices.

I

ICE CREAM

Many people associate ice cream with childhood feelings of happiness, innocence, and pleasure. But if ice cream appears in your dream, it may signify that you need to slow down and savor life. Ice cream can also indicate the need for comfort—are you in need of a little more sweetness in your life?

ICE SKATING

Did you enjoy ice skating when you were a child? If so, dreaming of ice skating may signify fun and laughter. If you were afraid of losing your balance and falling over, however, it suggests a fear that you're skating on thin ice and need to find more steadiness in life.

IDENTICAL TWINS

If you see identical twins in your dream it may signify a strong bond or connection. Perhaps you have met someone and the similarities between you are uncanny? An alternative interpretation is that you are not being authentic; you are trying too hard to be like someone else. Embrace your uniqueness.

INDECISION

Dreaming of indecisiveness suggests a lack of confidence or being pulled in opposite directions. This may reflect a doubt or dilemma in waking life. Tune into your intuition and be guided by your heart.

INDIGESTION

If you struggle with indigestion in your dream, it suggests something is bothering you or making you feel uneasy. Are you finding something emotionally hard to digest?

INJECTION

Dreaming of receiving an injection indicates you feel the need to be uplifted or healed in some way. It can also be associated with creative ideas or new relationships. Reflect on the person doing the injecting. Who are they? Are they injecting something positive or negative?

ISLAND

A desert island may seem like a dreamy place but if there is no means of escape then it can soon turn into a nightmare. It may suggest that you have a feeling or fear of being trapped in your life—perhaps you are in a relationship with an overbearing partner or maybe your job is limiting and stale. This dream is a call to arms, to make changes so that you can soar.

ITCH

Do you dream of an itch that you just can't scratch? If so, you may need to grab the bull by the horns and do that thing you've been itching to do all these years. Itches in dreams suggest yearnings or irritations that need to be soothed.

JELLYFISH

A jellyfish in your dream may represent buried feelings floating to the surface. Jellyfish sting any animal that is seen as a threat, so you may be feeling the need to protect yourself. Alternatively, this dream could be warning you that you are unnecessarily sharp with people.

JEWELERY

Pay close attention to the jewelery in your dream as it often reflects your sense of self-worth. Precious stones are associated with lasting beauty, whereas costume jewelery, or wearing too much jewelery, suggests that you are trying too hard to impress others. Make sure your feelings of beauty and worth come from within.

JIGSAW PUZZLE

No prizes for guessing that jigsaw puzzles in dreams represent putting something together or solving a problem. If your piece does not fit, you may be struggling to find your place in the world, or you may fear there is something missing in your life. Don't fret: the missing piece is probably right under your nose!

JOB

Dreaming of losing your job is not necessarily a bad sign. Your job represents your talents and how you contribute to the world. This dream may be flagging the fact that you have more to give or that you need to do work you are passionate about. Dreaming of quitting your job suggests you are giving up on yourself (or you really do hate your job and can't wait to resign).

JUMPING

If you jump in your dream, this can indicate a desire to take a risk or a big step towards a goal. If you are afraid to jump, something may be holding you back in real life. It could be uncertainty or fear of change. The clue lies in how the jump makes you feel. If you're jumping for joy, happy days!

JUNGLE

A tropical jungle can represent our subconscious: the wild, instinctual part of ourselves. The wild animals we encounter in our dreams may be old memories and emotions that need to be dealt with. Watch out for crocodiles!

JUNK FOOD

If you tuck into some junk food in your dream, you may not be taking good care of your physical or emotional needs in real life. Slow down and take the time to nourish your mind, body, and spirit.

JUSTICE

Dreaming about justice suggests that you have been treated unfairly and feel the need to set something right. Now may be a good time to seize the reins and make some changes in your life.

Dream fact

Mary Shelley was inspired to write *Frankenstein* after experiencing a terrifying dream about a corpse that came back to life.

Dreams are the royal road to the unconscious.

—Sigmund Freud

KANGAROO

Kangaroos are known for the pouches in which they carry their young. Dreaming of a kangaroo may reflect your maternal or paternal instincts. Do you need to nurture someone, or are you being too protective? Try to remember what was inside the pouch. This may help you decode your dream's message.

KEYS

To dream of a key could indicate that you are opening up to new ideas or opportunities in your life. Changes could be afoot. If you are locking something in your dream, you may be repressing emotions or hiding something from others. If you have recently lost or misplaced something in your life, pay attention: your dream may be showing you where it is.

KISSING

To dream of kissing someone can reflect your feelings for this person—either romantic or platonic. If this doesn't make sense to you, then look at the qualities this person possesses. Is there anything about them that you admire? Sometimes kissing indicates a desire for a closer relationship with these aspects of yourself.

Dream fact

The dreamcatcher is a well-known Native American symbol. It is a hoop loosely woven with a web-like pattern and decorated with sacred objects. The dreamcatcher is believed to catch our nightmares and only allows the good dreams to pass through.

KITE

Kites can symbolize staying grounded while you pursue your dreams. You may have high ambitions but need to keep your feet on the ground. Kites are also associated with childlike fun, so it might be worth considering whether you need more of this in your life. Perhaps it's time to go outside and take your kite for a spin.

KNEE

While dreaming of knees can represent a physical issue, knees can also symbolize emotional support and the ability to move forward in life. Reflect on the condition of your knee in the dream—was it healthy or injured? See if there are any parallels in your waking life—are you feeling stuck or taking steps to move forward?

KNITTING

If you are knitting in your dream, or watching someone knitting, you may benefit from more community and creativity in your life. Think about what knitting symbolizes for you. Are you craving more tranquillity? Or do you associate knitting with a particular person? If so, reflecting on this person's qualities might help you unravel your dream.

KNOCKING

If you are knocking in your dream, this may indicate a desire to be welcomed into a group or family. By knocking, you are asking permission to enter. Knocking can also signify a new venture or opportunity.

KNOT

Seeing a knot in your dream suggests that you are feeling "tied up" or stuck in some way. If you are untying a knot in your dream, however, you may have the ability to solve complex problems and, if you persevere, a solution may soon be on its way.

Dream fact

Salvador Dalí, a master of surrealist art, was often inspired by the things he saw as he was drifting off to sleep. He would put a tin plate beside his chair and hold a key above it; as soon as he fell asleep he would wake himself with the noise of the key hitting the plate and then jot down his dreams, which he would reproduce in his artwork.

I am
certain of
nothing
but... the truth
of the
Imagination.

—John Keats

LABORATORY

Laboratories are places of experimentation and creation. It may be that you are currently trying out some new beliefs and ideas, or you are testing a new relationship. Alternatively, you may be going through a period of transformation. Study the laboratory for clues—what is being tested, who is the scientist at work, and what is the conclusion of their experiment?

LADDER

Ladders in dreams can symbolize reaching career or spiritual heights. Have you just achieved a promotion at work or started a new meditation practice? If you are climbing a ladder in your dream, try to remember which rung you were on—each rung may represent a stage in your journey.

LANDSCAPE

If you see a landscape in your dream, try to remember if it is one you are familiar with in waking life. If so, you may be longing to go back there or to experience the feelings you associate with the area. The sort of landscape you're looking at may reflect different psychological states. Is the land barren and deserted (symbolizing loneliness, possibly) or teeming with lush, green plants (symbolizing abundance and riches)?

LATE

Dreaming that you are running late for a meeting or appointment can reflect your own lack of time management in real life, or it could signify that you are struggling to juggle all your priorities. What event did you arrive late for in your dream? Sometimes arriving late can reflect your subconscious resistance to something or someone.

LAWN

With their pristine grass, lawns symbolize image and appearance. They can also signify your overall health and well-being. If your lawn is overgrown and full of weeds, it may be time to make some adjustments to your lifestyle, such as eating more healthily, taking up regular exercise, and being more mindful to your physical and emotional needs.

LEFTOVERS

To see or eat leftovers in your dream may mean you are still clinging to something and it's time to let go. It can also mean that there is something in real life that you can reuse. Think about what was left over in your dream and then consider what you are going to do with any leftovers you may have (physical or mental) in your life.

LETTER

Receiving or writing a letter in your dream may indicate someone is trying to tell you something in real life or you feel the need to say something to someone. There's also the possibility that the letter is guidance from your subconscious. It may have been trying to tell you something for quite some time and now it has put its message in a letter.

LIBRARY

Libraries have strong associations with knowledge and information. Are you searching for something? Do you have a hunger for ideas? Libraries can also represent emotions and memories. If you were searching for a particular book, the title of the book and/or its condition may be significant.

LIGHT BULB

Dreaming of a light bulb may indicate greater insight or an "aha!" moment. It may also suggest you are at a point in your life where you can see things more clearly and feel ready to accept a situation or face reality. If the light is dull or the light bulb has burned out, however, it could symbolize a fear that you are running out of ideas or energy. Maybe a new approach will shed some light on the situation.

Did you know...?

Although dreams in literature are technically not dreams—as they were penned while the author was in a state of consciousness—they are a popular subject of analysis. Here are some of the most well-known literary dream sequences:

★ *Alice's Adventures in Wonderland*—From the moment Alice falls down the rabbit hole, the entire plot is set in a dream-like world. This meant Lewis Carroll could really bend the rules of convention in his story.

★ *Iliad*—This epic poem by Homer comprises a false dream imagined by Zeus. This is strong evidence that even ancient Greeks were as intrigued by the impact of dreams as we are.

★ *A Midsummer Night's Dream*—The forest setting in Shakespeare's play acts as the transitional fantasy world where the impossible can happen.

MACHINE

Seeing a machine in your dream can reflect feelings of numbness. Are you mindlessly doing the same things over and over again? If so, this dream may be a warning that you need to break the boring pattern and get in touch with your feelings and passions. Machinery can also represent your body and how well it functions. A fit, healthy body should run like a well-oiled machine.

MAGGOTS

Dreaming of maggots may not strike you as being an especially good sign, and you'd be right; maggots are associated with things spoiling or going bad. Is there a relationship or venture that is well past its sell-by date? Is something eating away at you? If so, it's time to chuck out the rubbish and make space for fresh, new things.

MAGIC

If you dream of performing magic, you might be looking for more synchronicity and wonder in your life.

This dream may also reflect the fact that you recognize that you are your own magician; you have the power to manifest your life exactly as you wish!

MAGPIE

Magpies are associated with superstition. Consider the old saying, "One for sorrow, for two joy…" How many magpies were there in your dream? On the other hand, magpies are highly intelligent birds, so dreaming of them can represent inner knowing and self-reflection. You may be figuring out who you are and what your purpose is right now.

MAP

If you see a map in your dream, you may be searching for direction in your life. You may be on the road to self-discovery—tuning into your life's purpose. If you are lost or don't know which way to turn, look to see if there is something different or unusual about the map which might give you a clue as to which path to take next.

MARATHON

Dreaming of running a marathon suggests that there may be a particular situation in your life that is asking you to grit your teeth. Try to keep going until you reach the finish line.

MASSAGE

Dreaming of a massage suggests you are in need of nurture and TLC. Are you holding on to unnecessary tension? Do you need to let go? Reflect on who is giving and receiving the massage. Your dream could be telling you that you need to take care of your body or inject more sensuality into your relationship.

MAZE

If you dream of being lost in a maze, you might be confused by the twists and turns of real life. Perhaps you struggle to deal with your jumbled thoughts and emotions? If you think the maze in your dream may reflect a real situation, think about how the maze was portrayed in your dream. Can you see anything that might signal a way out?

MEETING A CELEBRITY

To dream that you meet a celebrity, especially one that you are attracted to in real life, suggests that you are idealizing a relationship and are likely to be disappointed when things don't work out as hoped. To dream of befriending a celebrity denotes that you have a friend who has a propensity to behave like a bit of a prima donna; alternatively, it can mean that you're feeling a bit too much on the periphery of your social circle and want to be more popular.

Dream fact

Toddlers do not feature in their own dreams until they are around three to four years old.

MONEY

Money in dreams can represent your finances, your self-worth, or your feelings of abundance. Ask yourself how the money made you feel and where it came from: winning it indicates success and good fortune are within reach; finding it portents to your search for love, whereas losing it alludes to a recent setback in your life or that you've lost interest in something that was once dear to you. From a practical point of view, this dream may be reminding you about a bill that needs to be paid!

I want to keep my dreams, even bad ones, because without them I might have nothing all night long.

—Joseph Heller

CARL JUNG
(1875-1961)

Carl Jung, a Swiss psychoanalyst, was the founder of analytical psychology and a close follower and friend of Sigmund Freud. Although he often collaborated with Freud throughout his career, he diverged from Freud's belief that neuroses had a sexual basis. Instead, Jung advanced his own theories around dreaming and the power of the unconscious.

The key idea behind Jungian dream theory was that dreams revealed more than they concealed; Jung theorized that as dreams were a natural expression of our imagination, they used a simple language, such as mythic narratives, to express their meaning. Jung did not believe that dreams needed to be interpreted, but that their function was to integrate our conscious and unconscious lives; this process was called individuation.

Jung also proposed the idea that there was a collective unconscious, rather than only a personal unconscious, from which certain universal patterns and symbols have arisen throughout history. By this, Jung didn't mean that there was some kind of telepathic reservoir of knowledge, but that the psychological constants in society like marriage and puberty mean that all humans have elements of a shared unconscious. Jung believed that the role of a psychotherapist was to help an individual create their own personal mythology so that they could understand their dreams better and relate them to their waking life.

NAKED

Being naked is a common dream theme, which can signify feeling vulnerable and exposed in real life. Your naked self may symbolize who you are deep down inside. If you are enjoying the feeling of being naked among other people, however, you are either very comfortable in your own skin or you have an extrovert side to you which needs to be unleashed! Being without clothes can also symbolize a breaking down of barriers, as clothes themselves are a layer of protection. It could be that you need to let your guard down and show your vulnerability in order to enhance your connection with an individual or situation.

NAP

If you dream about taking a nap you probably need to take some time off and relax, or perhaps take a break from a particular area of your life.

NECK

Necks can represent how flexible we are in a situation. If your neck is stiff and sore in your dream, your views about someone or something may be too rigid. Necks can also represent the mind–body connection. Are you listening to your heart? An alternative interpretation is that someone is being a pain in the neck!

NEEDING
THE TOILET

This common dream of being caught short alludes to pent-up emotions that need to be released. It could also mean that you have outgrown someone or something and it's time to distance yourself from them, or you need to shed your inhibitions to move forward and feel happy in your own skin. Seeing toilet paper in a dream denotes emotional release and the need for a period of self-evaluation and healing.

Dream fact

In 1886, Robert Louis Stevenson dreamed up three key scenes in *The Strange Case of Dr. Jekyll and Mr. Hyde.*

NEWSPAPER

If you see a newspaper in your dream, you may be the sort of person who likes to be well informed. If you can remember, reflect on what the headlines were and how you reacted. Was your paper full of good or bad news? If your paper was full of negative headlines, this may reflect your fears and anxieties in the real world.

NOMAD

Dreaming of living a nomadic life suggests you yearn for more freedom and adventure. It could also mean that you feel at home in lots of different situations. A third option to consider is that you frequently change your mind and could do with settling on one thing.

NOSE

Noses are how we sense things we sometimes cannot see. Dreaming of the nose can therefore represent your intuition (do you follow your nose?). Noses can also represent energy and determination. You may be determined to complete a task or achieve a goal (i.e. you keep your nose to the grindstone).

NUMB

If a part of your body is numb in your dream, you may be feeling indifferent or disconnected from your emotions. You could also be feeling paralyzed and unable to move forward in some way. Look for clues in your dream—are you feeling cold or disconnected from a person, event, or situation?

NUMBER

If you see numbers in your dream, you may be a very logical, rational person. If you are working on a problem or challenge right now, try employing your analytical left brain to find a solution. Different numbers can also be personally significant. Do you feel a connection with the number in your dream? Does it represent a special age, date, or address? Or perhaps a lucky number on a lottery ticket?

NURSE

Dreaming about a nurse suggests you need to show compassion towards someone or you want someone to take care of you. This dream may also be nudging you to look after yourself so that your mind and body can heal. Consider the ways in which you care for other people or help them solve their problems. Could this be your new career?

OASIS

Seeing an oasis in your dream alludes to an area of your waking life that requires attention. However, if you reach the oasis, there is hope. Draw on your inner resources and keep putting one foot in front of the other. Your oasis may appear on the horizon sooner than you imagine.

OBEDIENCE

Dreaming about obeying someone may symbolize the acceptance of an authority figure or a lack of power in your waking life. Dreaming about being disobedient suggests a rebellious nature and a dislike of being bossed around. If someone is being obedient towards you, this reflects the influence you have over others.

Nights through dreams tell the myths forgotten by the day.

—Carl Jung

Dream fact

Studies have shown that animals dream and experience nightmares in much the same way as we do.

OBSESSION

If you are obsessed with someone or something in your dream, think about the qualities this person, place, or object possesses. Would you like to have these same qualities yourself? The strong feelings you have in the dream may be positive or negative, suggesting either a healthy admiration or a harmful addiction.

OCEAN

This symbol represents powerful thoughts and the bridge between your unconscious mind and your waking life. Dreaming of the ocean or a large body of water can help you to find ways of dealing with strong emotions. Try to recall how you felt in this dream and look for links to the physical world. Above all, this symbol serves as a reminder to seek what's in your heart and follow your dreams to fruition.

OCTOPUS

With its eight tentacles, an octopus represents entanglement. If one appears in your dream, you may have your hands full in real life or you may be involved in a tricky situation that you're struggling to get out of. You may also be too clingy in a relationship and need to give your partner some breathing space.

ORCHARD

A blooming orchard indicates that your life is full of abundance. If the orchard is bare or the fruit is rotten, it suggests you are oblivious to all the things you have to be grateful for. Use this dream to remind you to focus on the important things in life so that they flourish.

OWL

We often think of owls as being wise figures. However, owls can also represent the unconscious or your own animal energy. Is the owl imparting some message or insight? Practice trusting what your heart is telling you—you have a wise owl inside of you.

Dream fact

Research reveals that we sleep better during a new moon and worse during a full moon.

PACKAGE

If you receive a package in your dream, this could indicate that you are anticipating that something exciting is about to happen. It may also symbolize a desire to express hidden talents—instead of singing in the shower, it could be time to take center stage.

PADDLE

Dreaming of a paddle or an oar can reflect how you navigate through life. Are you steering well or struggling to stay on course? The way you paddle in your dream may also symbolize your ability to handle your emotions. Is your paddling calm and smooth or are you splashing about all over the place?

–P–

PAINTING

Dreaming about painting can mean that you long to express yourself creatively. But it can also point to the need for change. It depends on what's being painted and who is doing the painting. Dreaming about painting your house, for example, could mean that some aspect of your life could do with a makeover or you're covering up something you don't want others to see.

PALACE

If you dream of a palace or a mansion, you may be yearning for more luxury in your life. If you dream of living in a palace, success may be just around the corner.

PANTHER

Panthers in dreams can signify lurking danger or beauty, or power and courage. Ask yourself what the panther was doing in your dream and how it made you feel. Was the panther stalking you (watch out: someone may not have your best intentions at heart) or was it a protective presence?

PARACHUTE

Parachutes can represent security and protection. You may feel as if you have a caring force looking out for you. Alternatively, your dream may be warning you it's time to bail out of an old situation, idea, or habit. If your parachute doesn't open, you may feel let down or unprepared. You could be about to come down to earth with a bump!

PARALYSIS

Being paralyzed and unable to move is a common dream. It represents feeling helpless or stuck. You may suffer from recurring thoughts and actions that are causing you harm. To break the pattern and set yourself free, ask yourself: in what way do I feel paralyzed, and what is holding me back in my life?

PEGASUS

To dream of the mythical winged horse symbolizes fleetness of foot and agility, and that you will overcome your current difficulties.

All human beings are also dream beings. Dreaming ties all mankind together.

—Jack Kerouac

QUARANTINE

If you dream that you are placed in quarantine, ask yourself whether you need to distance yourself from a negative influence in your life, or whether you are cut off from some aspect of yourself.

QUARREL

Dreaming that you are quarrelling with someone may indicate that you have unresolved issues in your relationships or you may be struggling with inner conflict and turmoil. Think about who is quarrelling and what the quarrel is about.

QUAY

Dreaming of a quay or harbor can be a positive sign. It suggests you are moving towards a new chapter in your life. Lots of boats docked in the quay signifies the fulfilment of your dreams and wishes. On a more literal level, this dream may also reflect your urge to travel or test out your sea legs.

QUEEN (OR KING)

To dream of being a queen (or king) symbolizes a need for power and influence. If you feel overwhelmed by your royal responsibilities, however, it suggests you are taking on too much in real life. You have higher ambitions than you are able to handle. On a positive note, becoming a queen (or king) can indicate that you have spiritual, teaching, or leadership powers.

QUICKSAND

To dream that you are sinking in quicksand suggests you may not be standing on solid ground in real life. Perhaps you feel insecure or have misjudged a situation? Alternatively, you may not be being true to who you are. Is it time to make some changes and live a more congruent life?

QUITTING

Dreaming about quitting something isn't necessarily a bad sign. Quitting can be positive, as in the case of giving up smoking or ending an unhealthy relationship. Beware of making snap decisions (dreaming of quitting your job does not necessarily mean you should walk out) as symbols in dreams are not always meant to be taken literally. Look for areas in your life where an ending has just taken place or needs to take place.

How blessed are some people, whose lives have no fears, no dreads, to whom sleep is a blessing that comes nightly, and brings nothing but sweet dreams.

—Bram Stoker

RADIO

A dream that includes a radio represents information of
some kind. This could be information coming in from
an outside source, a message from your subconscious,
or even some sort of telepathic communication. You
may be acutely in tune with someone else or have an
intuitive grasp of a situation. If your radio is turned off,
are your frequencies blocked?

RAFT

Dreaming of a raft can symbolize your ability to stay afloat despite the chaos that surrounds you. Is your raft drifting on calm water or being thrown about by waves and rapids? If your raft still floats, bravo: you are able to stay in control despite your turbulent surroundings. (But watch out if you are just drifting through life.) If your raft is sinking or you have lost your oar, this could be an ominous sign.

RAINBOW

Seeing a rainbow in real life is always an uplifting experience. Rainbows in dreams represent hope, success, joy, and positivity. They can also represent spirituality and a connection to higher realms. If you're hoping for a pot of gold at the end of the rainbow, however, you could be indulging in wishful thinking!

RASH

Dreaming of a rash can indicate that something or someone is irritating you. It could even be something you once did or said. An alternative interpretation is that you are bottling up anger or frustration and need to let it out. Figure out what's bugging you and go and hit some pillows.

RECURRING DREAMS

Did you have a sense of déjà vu in your dream? Recurring dreams are often a sign that your subconscious is trying to tell you something important. Pay attention to the message in your dream. Is there a theme or pattern emerging? There may be an issue you need to resolve or some action you need to take in real life.

RING

Rings have obvious associations with marriage and commitment, but they can also symbolize emotional wholeness. If you see a ring on your finger in a dream, it may signify your commitment to a new endeavor or relationship.

ROOM

Rooms can refer to aspects of your physical health. The kitchen can refer to your digestive system, the bedroom to your reproductive system, the bathroom to your bowels, and so on. Think about how these aspects of your health are functioning as your unconscious mind may be alerting you to an undiagnosed health problem.

ROTTEN

Was there something rotten in your dream? This may represent a bad situation or person in your life. It could also mean that you are not nourishing yourself properly. Have you been neglecting your physical or emotional well-being? Figure out what the rotting object symbolizes and take steps to stop the rot (unless you feel the decay needs to run its course to allow the birth of a new stage in your life).

RUNNING

Dreaming about running can have all sorts of meanings depending on the context of the dream. What are you running from? Where are you running to? And how does the running make you feel? Your answers to these three questions can give you clues as to what your dream means. Are you running away from a problem in your life or are you running determinedly towards your goals and dreams, for example?

Did you know...?

Some of mankind's greatest ideas have derived from dreams, such as:

★ Google search engine—Larry Page
★ DNA's double-helix spiral—James Watson
★ The sewing machine—Elias Howe
★ The periodic table—Dmitri Mendeleev

SAFE
(OR VAULT)

A safe or vault can represent your feelings of self-worth and/or a desire for protection. Pay close attention to what you put in the safe. Does the symbol represent personal values that need to be honored or parts of your psyche that you want to protect? Is there a secret you want to keep hidden? An empty safe can signify loss or lack.

SALON

Dreaming of a hair or beauty salon may indicate the need for some TLC. Do you need to take better care of yourself and put your needs first for a while? It could be that you're trying too hard to impress other people. Or you simply had a bad hair day—things will look better tomorrow.

SALT

We add salt to enhance the flavor of our food, so dreaming of salt may reflect a need for more excitement in your life. Do you feel as if something is missing? Look for ways to add more flavor and spice to your life.

SCAB

If you see a scab in your dream, it may symbolize a period of healing for you. Perhaps you are recovering from a physical or emotional wound in real life? If you pick at the scab in your dream, it may be a sign that you need to relax, stop interfering, and let things take their natural course.

SCISSORS

Scissors represent cutting something out of your life. This could be something tangible like a friendship or a sweater you haven't worn for years. Or it could be something psychological such as an old belief that's been holding you back. Scissors also represent childhood, so it could be time to get the glue and glitter out and have a craft day.

SEAL

Seals are joyful, playful creatures. Seeing a seal in your dream may symbolize fun and laughter. Do you need more seal-like qualities in your everyday life? If your seal was performing in some way, do you have a deep-seated desire to entertain others? Think about what the seal was doing in your dream and see if you can draw any parallels with your waking life.

Dream fact

A pipe dream is typically associated with something that you will never achieve. This phrase can be traced back to the dreams experienced by opium smokers in the eighteenth and nineteenth centuries.

SKY

The complexion of the sky in your dream determines its meaning. If the sky is blue like a summer's day, it means that you are experiencing a moment of clarity, whereas an overcast sky can mean that your judgement is somewhat clouded and you could be feeling a little gloomy about a certain situation in your waking life.

SNAKES

Seeing snakes slithering in your dream means there is a slippery character in your life who can't be trusted. Another meaning is that a person has slipped out of your life and you are missing them.

Dream fact

There is a rare disorder called "sleeping beauty syndrome" in which the sufferer, usually in their adolescent years, cannot be woken up by another person once they are asleep. These episodes of sleep can last for days, weeks, and even months, and have been known to continue for up to ten years.

SPIDERS

To dream of a big, hairy tarantula is often a reference to a strong female figure in your life—maybe your mother-in-law? It also represents your darker side and that perhaps it's time to reveal something about yourself that you have kept under wraps for too long.

SPOTS

A breakout of spots or acne can mean that you are worried that you are not living up to someone's expectations or even meeting the standards that you have set yourself. It's time to be kinder to yourself and create achievable steps towards your goals.

CALVIN S. HALL
(1909–1985)

A follower of the Freudian method, Calvin S. Hall was an American psychologist who specialized in the field of dream research and analysis. Hall began his research on dreams in the 1940s and wrote a number of books on the topic, including primers in both Freudian and Jungian psychology.

Since Hall believed that dreams were essentially just thoughts we had while sleeping, he proposed that dreams were a cognitive process. Hall theorized—like some of his psychological predecessors—that dreams provided a route into the unreachable parts of your psyche, and so were the best way of discovering your inner thoughts and explaining your behavior. Following from these ideas, Hall categorized dreams into five

principal concepts: self, others, the world, penalties, and conflicts.

Undoubtedly, Hall's most significant innovation in dream research was his development of a content analysis system for dreams. Alongside psychologist Robert Van de Castle, Hall developed a scale that scored dream reports against 16 empirical scales, ranging all the way from mythical creatures to sexual encounters. This scale was a huge milestone in the scientific study of dreams, allowing researchers up to the present day to gain a statistically significant snapshot of dreaming cognition.

TABLE

Tables are places we gather around with friends and family—so a table in your dream could symbolize your relationships. If there are people sitting at the table, look at how they interact—this could reveal how you feel about your relationships in waking life. A broken table suggests your relationships are in need of repair.

TALENT SHOW

Dreaming that you are in a talent show indicates that you're aware of your potential and you are heading towards a new stage in life. A happy, clapping audience suggests you have a good network of people to support you. If you dream that you are watching a talent show, are your unique gifts going to waste in real life?

TATTOO

Tattoos in dreams can have various meanings depending on what the tattoo depicts and where it is located. Tattoos generally symbolize self-expression and a desire to stand out from the crowd, but they can also represent permanency—something that can't be undone in the future. Examine your tattoo for clues as to why it might have special significance for you.

TEACHER

To dream that you are a teacher indicates that you have gained wisdom and knowledge that you can now pass on to others. If you are learning from a teacher, it suggests you have things left to learn and accomplish in some aspect of your life.

TEETH
FALLING OUT

To dream of your teeth rotting and falling out suggests you have let something slip that you now regret. It could be that you have been spreading rumors or telling lies. Other interpretations of this common dream are that you are embarrassed about something or you have a feeling of powerlessness in your waking life. One positive interpretation is that it signifies money coming your way—perhaps the tooth fairy is about to pay you a visit?

TELEPHONE

If a telephone features in your dream, you may need to speak to someone in real life—perhaps an old friend you have lost touch with, or someone you need to say something important to. If you receive a phone call, listen to the message very carefully. A constantly ringing phone implies there's a message you're not paying attention to.

Dream fact

Daydreaming is an altered state of consciousness, much like when we sleep. Psychologists tell us that daydreaming happens when we carry our dreams with us; whatever we are daydreaming about can be linked to what we were dreaming of when we were asleep.

TEST

Sitting for an exam or a test is a common dream, which can reveal deep-seated fears about success and failure. Passing a test can indicate that you are ready for what life might throw at you. Failing a test may symbolize feeling insecure or inadequate in some way. Do you have a test coming up in real life? You'd better knuckle down to some revision!

TORNADO

If you see a tornado in your dream, it could be a sign of emotional outbursts and anger issues. Perhaps you are in a volatile relationship or a situation in which you feel out of control? The tornado or whirlwind may be a metaphor for destructive habits or behaviors—in yourself or others.

TRAPDOOR

A trapdoor in a dream, whether you fall through it or not, means something unexpected is about to happen in your life.

TURNING
(SOMETHING) OFF

Dreaming of turning something off suggests that you no longer need something in your life or you feel cut off in some way—from yourself, your friends, or family. Examine what you are turning off. What qualities and emotions do you associate with this object? If the above interpretations don't ring true, you may have forgotten to turn the oven off!

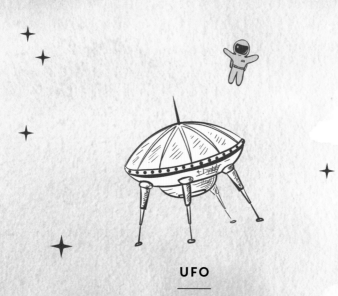

UFO

If your dream involves little green men and UFOs, you may be ready to explore a new or alien territory, or perhaps to find your spiritual purpose in life. Alternatively, you may be feeling alienated or "spaced out." Dreaming of UFOs can simply mean that you are speculating about something that is currently unknown to you; for example, you could have a job interview on the horizon or a date, and you're not sure how to approach it as you can't foresee how the situation will develop. See *Alien*.

UMBRELLA

If you see an umbrella in your dream, try to remember whether it was open or closed. An open umbrella can symbolize your desire to put up a shield to protect yourself from feeling emotions. A closed umbrella can reflect your willingness to feel and express your emotions fully.

UNDERWATER

To dream that you are underwater suggests that you feel "in over your head" regarding a situation or relationship. You may be feeling overwhelmed or overcome with emotions. It's a very different matter, however, if you find yourself able to breathe underwater and swim around freely. This suggests you are in control of your emotions as you ride the waves of life!

UNDERWEAR

Underwear represents the parts of yourself that you keep hidden from others, so it's important to reflect on the condition of your underwear for clues as to what your dream may mean. Torn or tattered underwear can indicate you think poorly of yourself, whereas beautiful, luxurious underwear suggests a positive self-image. Is this dream a subtle message from your subconscious that it's high time you upgraded your undies?

UNICORN

If you see one of these fantastical beasts in your dream, you may be longing for more magic in your life. Unicorns represent imagination, childhood, hope, and innocence. If you see one, it's generally a good omen (less so if you see one in real life).

UPSTAIRS

Were you going upstairs in your dream? If so, this indicates an interest in spirituality or higher states of consciousness. Your feelings towards these topics may be reflected in the stairs themselves. If the stairs in your dream are incomplete and some treads are missing, it means that you are cutting corners (missing a few steps) in your attempts to achieve your goals, and tripping up on the stairs means that you're not ready to confront repressed feelings.

U-TURN

Doing a U-turn in a dream can symbolize a great turning point in your life. You may be about to change direction and start down a completely new path. Of course, it could also mean you've made a wrong decision and need to backtrack pretty fast.

VACUUM

To see an empty space suggests feelings of emptiness—perhaps a piece of the jigsaw is missing in your life? It could be that a relationship isn't going as well as hoped or you're not finding fulfilment in your work. Take steps now to populate your life with good things, write a list of goals, and reconnect with people that make you happy when you're with them.

VAMPIRE

To dream about vampires suggests that either you are sucking the life force out of someone or they are draining the life out of you! This can happen in myriad ways—from small judgements and put-downs to in-your-face anger. If you know someone is bad for you, take steps to protect yourself. And if you're the one with your fangs out, try to rein it in a little.

VASE

If the vase in your dream is ornate or fancy, you may be craving the limelight in real life If it contains flowers, this could represent putting yourself, or some object, on display for all to see. Another interpretation on seeing flowers in a vase is that you want to keep your life small or contained in some way, rather than allowing yourself to be wild and free.

VEGETABLE GARDEN

A vegetable garden represents self-sufficiency. If you dream of growing your own food, you are a self-reliant and capable person. This dream is hinting that you have everything you need within you to create a fantastic life. You just need to shower yourself with love and care... and eat your five a day!

VEHICLE

Consider what the vehicle looks like: is it sleek and new or scratched and dented? Vehicles represent how you are moving through life, and the mode of transport and its roadworthiness are indicators as to whether your situation is stable or requires an inspection of sorts—perhaps you need to brush up on your skills by signing up to a course in order to proceed to the next career level, or your nearest and dearest needs a bit of TLC? See *Driving*.

VERMIN

To dream of vermin means that something undesirable has entered your life. It could be a person but it's equally likely that a negative character trait has resurfaced—perhaps you're more short-tempered than usual or you've recently become a bit of a grump? It's time to iron out those less appealing traits as they could be holding you back from achieving your full potential.

VOLCANO

As you might expect, a volcano can represent suppressed rage. Is there an issue from the past that's starting to rear its head again? Can you feel your anger building? Volcanos can also be a sign of positive things inside us that are waiting to come out—creativity or new depths of self-knowledge, for example. Volcanos can be powerful symbols of transformation.

VOMITING

Being sick in a dream can quite literally mean you can't stomach someone or something a second longer. On an emotional level, vomiting in a dream can symbolize the need to expel negative beliefs or ideas that have been harming you. Is it time to dump that relationship or job? Or simply declutter your wardrobe?

Even a *soul* submerged in sleep is hard at work and *helps* make something of the *world.*

—Heraclitus

WAIST

An obvious interpretation of seeing a waist in your dream is that you are concerned about your diet or weight. However, the dream may also be a pun on wasting time or money or some other item in your life. Some dreams have a warped sense of humor.

WALKING STICK

Do you feel supported? A walking stick may reflect your need for help in some area of your life. Don't be afraid to reach out to other people for assistance and advice.

WALL

A wall in your dream signifies obstacles in your path. If you scale the wall easily, however, it is a prediction of future success. Building a wall could be a sign that you are trying to protect yourself from getting hurt. Dreaming of a wall with a "keep out" sign or security fencing means you must break down your self-imposed barriers in order to move forward.

WART

If you dream you have a wart, there's no need to be unduly concerned; it signifies you will become rich! Warts on others are not such a fortuitous sign—they signify hidden hostility.

WASHING MACHINE

Seeing or using a washing machine in your dream suggests you need to let go of past issues and make a fresh start. What feelings, beliefs or relationships are holding you back in your life? Out with the old and in with the new.

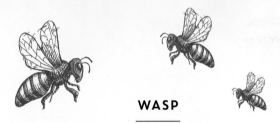

WASP

Dreaming of wasps suggests that you are feeling tormented by hardships, conflict, and setbacks in your life. You may be feeling "stung" by others' words or taken advantage of in some way. Dreaming of killing a wasp signifies your willingness to stand up to those who are attacking you.

WATER

Water has different meanings depending on the context of the dream. Playing in water suggests you long for more fun in your life. Boiling water suggests emotional turmoil—you need to let off some steam. Calm, clear water denotes serenity and peace of mind—you are in tune with your spirituality. Muddy water indicates you are wallowing in negativity—it could be time to wash off the mud and give your emotions a spring clean.

WINNING AN AWARD

To dream of receiving a medal or an award, like an Oscar or a Nobel prize, suggests quite plainly that you would like to be honored for your achievements in your waking life. Perhaps it's time to drop a few hints about that bonus or promotion.

WINNING THE LOTTERY

This classic dream of abundance suggests that you need to conserve your resources and energies, rather than being a portent to riches. It may also be highlighting that you are lacking something—this could be either a physical or spiritual "thing." Another interpretation is that it signifies a happy event—maybe you should nip to the corner shop for a lottery ticket after all!

Dream fact

Research shows that 70 percent of the time men have dreams about other men, while women dream about both sexes equally.

Our
imagination
flies—
we are its
shadow
on
the earth.

—Vladimir Nabokov

X

An "X" appearing in your dream may represent something that is forbidden or that needs to be cut out of your life. Look for areas in your life where you are not allowed to do something, or where you've messed up and need to make amends. If your "X" appears in the middle of a treasure map, this is a different kettle of fish altogether. Your goals are in sight and you will soon be reaping some big rewards.

X-RAY

If you wake from a dream about having an X-ray, ask yourself which part of the body was involved—there may be a health issue that needs to be resolved. X-rays can also indicate a desire to learn more about your inner psyche or reveal your true emotions, like declaring your undying love for a special someone, for example.

Dream fact

It is said that within five minutes of being awake, 50 percent of our dream is forgotten, and within ten minutes, 90 percent has disappeared from our memory. However, if someone wakes us up while we are dreaming, we are more likely to remember it.

XYLOPHONE

Seeing a xylophone in your dream indicates a connection to, or concern for, the environment. A xylophone is a percussion instrument that is made with wooden panels. Playing a xylophone may signify a need for harmony, beauty, and nature in your life.

Did you know...?

Even the most logical of scientists are dreamers. Check out some of the greatest scientific theories that were literally dreamed up:

★ Niels Bohr's inspirational dream led to the discovery of the structure of the atom. Nothing he thought of was making sense, until he fell asleep and dreamed of the nucleus of an atom with electrons spinning around it. His vision of atomic structure became one of the greatest scientific breakthroughs.

★ Einstein discovered the theory of relativity after having a vivid dream. Einstein envisaged himself sliding down a mountainside so fast that he was traveling at the speed of light. The speed at which he was going meant that the stars in his dream changed their appearance in relation to him. He worked on this idea and eventually came up with his revolutionary scientific theory.

YACHT

If you see a yacht in your dream, it's probably a very good sign. Yachts symbolize wealth and luxury. Your dream may mean that you are free of worry or that it would be a good idea to put your feet up for a while.

 ## YARN

Dreaming about yarn could represent a yearning to create something from scratch—a Christmas sweater or a pair of mittens, perhaps. Yarn can also represent playfulness (e.g. a kitten playing with a ball of yarn). If your yarn is tangled, however, it means your emotions are in a knot.

YAWNING

Yawning in a dream is an obvious sign that you are lacking in energy, or are in need of emotional or intellectual stimulation.

YELLOW

The color yellow is associated with joy and happiness. Dreaming about this color implies you are feeling hopeful for the future or that you are intuitively picking up on blessings that will soon be appearing in your life. If your dream is unpleasant, yellow may signify jealousy or cowardice. However, sometimes dreams are more straightforward than this—perhaps you're just not keen on the color yellow!

YES

"Yes" symbolizes acceptance of a condition, situation, or decision. Dreaming about saying "yes" to something could be a sign that you need to go ahead and do that thing you've been having doubts about in your waking life... Are you still here? What are you waiting for? Go for it!

YOGA

Dreaming about doing yoga, or seeing a yogi in your dream, can mean different things depending on what yoga signifies to you. Maybe you need to pay more attention to your body and physical health? Or perhaps you need to lead a simpler, more spiritual life? Thinking about the qualities you associate with yoga can help you to interpret what your dream is trying to tell you.

YOLK

The yellow yolk of an egg nourishes the developing embryo. An egg yolk in your dream could indicate that you need to take steps to look after yourself or become more independent. Of course, new life hatches from eggs. So egg yolks can also represent new ideas and creativity. Surely this is the perfect excuse to eat more eggs for breakfast.

YOUNG

If you see young people in your dream, this may reflect a new fresh outlook on life or a desire to be playful and carefree. If you dream that you are young again, watch out: you may be behaving childishly and could do with maturing in one or two areas of your life.

YO-YO

Yo-yos signify the ups and downs of life. Playing with a yo-yo in your dream may be a strong sign that your emotions are all over the place or that you are not taking your problems seriously enough. On a more positive note, yo-yos can represent a desire for the simpler pleasures in life. Buy yourself a yo-yo and enjoy!

NORMAN MALCOLM
(1911–1990)

Born in a tiny town in Kansas, Norman Malcolm went on to study philosophy at the University of Nebraska, Harvard, and the University of Cambridge in his later life. Malcolm was a contemporary and close friend of fellow philosopher Ludwig Wittgenstein, who had a major impact on his way of thinking. Both men subscribed closely to the "ordinary language" philosophy, and Malcolm soon developed his own ideas on the concept of dreaming and the problems that stemmed from its traditional expression in psychological discourse.

Malcolm argued in his paper *Dreaming and Skepticism* (1956) and his book *Dreaming* (1959) that the notion of dreams, in the sense of conscious experiences that have both a definite time and duration, was an "unintelligible" concept. At its heart, his philosophy proposed that it was only through our own descriptions of dreaming at the

point of waking up that we could account for the dream taking place; because of this, we can't verify what someone really dreamed, or whether they dreamed at all. Although Malcolm was not trying to argue that dreams didn't exist, he put forward the idea that we needed to re-evaluate our shared concept of dreaming, since it is so closely tied to the "waking reports" of dreams and not to verifiable evidence.

ZEBRA

A zebra appearing in your dream could reflect your ability to see both sides of an argument. On the other hand, it could indicate black-and-white thinking. To figure out which one it is, ask yourself whether there are areas in your life where your thinking could be more flexible, or where you need to find a way to balance extremes.

ZEN

Dreaming of being Zen—at peace with yourself— symbolizes your desire for tranquillity and simplicity. Perhaps it's time to take up yoga or meditation?

ZIPPER

Zippers are full of sexual innuendo. If you dream about unzipping a zipper, it could mean that you are opening up emotionally or to new sexual experiences. Zipping up a zipper suggests that you are shutting down emotionally or simply that you need to stop talking and keep your mouth zipped!

ZOMBIE

Dreaming that you are a zombie may not be the most auspicious sign. It suggests you may be feeling "dead" inside or that you lack passion and purpose in your life. Dreaming of being attacked by zombies could be a sign that you are feeling overwhelmed in your work or home life. Find ways to inject more fun into your days. And steer clear of graveyards at night!

ZOO

Unsurprisingly, zoos symbolize a loss of freedom. Do you feel trapped or cut off from your natural state in some way? Zoos are often busy and crowded places, so an alternative interpretation is that you're experiencing some chaos or confusion in your life. Perhaps it's time to take it easy, like a sloth.

ZOOMORPHISM

Do you take the form of an animal in your dream? If so, this may indicate that you are becoming more uninhibited and intuitive. It may also mean you are experiencing new-found freedom. A third option is that you have animal instincts that need to be expressed (yes, *that* sort!).

INDEX